Malayalam Alphabet

Practice Workbook

John D. Kunnathu

&

Lissy John

Copyright © 2017 John D. Kunnathu
All rights reserved.
ISBN:
ISBN-13:978-1981126514

John D. Kunnathu is an educator and an author of several books. He has had his higher studies in Language, Linguistics, Literature, Instructional Technology, and in Religious Studies.

Lissy John is an educator and a writer. She has had her higher studies in Language, Linguistics, and Literature. After being in Africa and in the US for over twenty-five years, both are now settled in Kerala.

They have also authored:
Speak Malayalam in Ten Weeks
Learn Basic Malayalam in Six weeks

Contact: johnkunnathu@gmail.com

How To Use This Book

This is a workbook for those who learn to write Malayalam Alphabet. The focus is on the shape of the letters, and on how to write them. The letters are ordered from simple to complex, so that the learners won't be intimidated by the few complex ones. The letters are classified into base forms, short forms, and combined forms.

A page is devoted for each letter. At the top left you see the letter along with the direction as to how to write it. A star indicates the place to start writing a letter. At the top right you see a little help as to its sound. Also you see a few words in which the letter occurs.

Then you see in six rows six sets of the letter in dotted lines in varying sizes. The biggest ones are at the top, and they become smaller as they go down. The learner is not supposed to write all of them together. In the first week, the learner may write only the ones in the first row. He/she may visit as many pages as time permits, but he/she should stay within the first row. In the second week, he/she may come back and do the second row of each of those pages he/she visited. Thus the learner needs to spend a minimum of six weeks to complete the entire book.

If the learner is a child, he/she should be directed to stick to the plan of one row per week. Filling each page fully before going to the next won't serve the purpose.

As the learner writes a letter, he/she needs to sound it too, so that each letter will be associated with the sound it represents. All Malayalam sounds don't have English equivalents. The learner will have to seek the help of a native speaker if available. The learner may also search in Youtube for Malayalam alphabet pronunciation, and listen from there.

There is also a list of a few common words and a few sentences toward the end of the book.

This is the very first book a level 1 learner of Malayalam may use. The same authors have made two more books available for the next levels. *Learn Basic Malayalam in Six Weeks* is level 2, and *Speak Malayalam in Ten Weeks* is level 3.

The Primary Difference between English and Malayalam Alphabet

You already know English, and naturally you might assume that the Malayalam alphabet is like that of English. Although they are similar in many ways, there is a big difference, which you need to be aware of before proceeding any further.

We speak and hear a language with the sounds produced from our mouth. Representing these sounds, we make some marks, the alphabet, on a paper using which we read and write language.

There are two kinds of sounds in every language-- vowels and consonants. Vowels come out of our mouth smoothly without any obstruction or constriction, but consonants come out with obstruction and constriction. Vowels are marked in the same way in both English and Malayalam except for one vowel-- the sound of 'A'. In Malayalam, this sound is marked only if it stands alone as a syllable-- അ. If it stands with a consonant, it is not marked; it remains invisible.

Malayalam	English script
കര	kara
കരി	kari
കുരി	kuri
കോരി	kori

In the above examples, all vowels are marked except the sound of 'A'. All consonant letters have the sound of 'A' attached, unless another vowel is specifically marked.

If you want to indicate that a consonant does not have the sound of 'A' attached with it, you have to mark it in some way. One way is to use a half-moon sign as in കട്. Another way is to use a short form for the second of the two consonants as in ക്ര. A third way is to modify the letter as ം, ൻ, ൽ, ൾ, ർ, and ൺ. Words in Malayalam end only in these modified letters or vowel sounds. Words can end in consonant sounds like b, d, f, g, k, p, s, and t in English, but not in Malayalam.

Contents

How To Use This Book..3
The Base Forms..7
The Short Forms of Vowels..53
Stressed Consonants...67
Consonant Combinations..87
The Short Forms of Consonants............................... 117
Consonants without a Vowel.................................... 123
Let us Make Some Words... 131
Let us Write Some Sentences................................... 139

The Base Forms

The letters represent speech sounds. Speech sounds are classified into vowels and consonants based on how they are produced. Vowels are produced without any obstruction or constriction within our mouth, but consonants are produced with obstruction and constriction.

Speech sounds combine to form syllables. A syllable is made of one vowel sound. It can also have one or more optional consonants.

Vowels

അ   ഇ   ഉ   എ   ഒ   ഋ

ആ   ഈ   ഊ   ഏ   ഓ

ഐ   ഔ

The ones in the first row are short; the ones in the second row are long, The ones in the third row are vowel combinations.

Consonants

ക	ഖ	ഗ	ഘ	ങ
ച	ഛ	ജ	ഝ	ഞ
ട	ഠ	ഡ	ഢ	ണ
ത	ഥ	ദ	ധ	ന
പ	ഫ	ബ	ഭ	മ

All consonant letters represent its consonant sound as well as the vowel sound of 'A' unless another vowel is marked.

യ   ര   ല   വ

ശ   ഷ   സ   ഹ

ള   ഴ   റ

Given Order

റ, ന, ത, വ, ര, ട, ഗ, ശ, ധ, ഠ, പ, ച, ദ, ഭ, ഫ, ഥ, ഹ, ല, മ, ഖ, ണ, ഒ, ഉ, സ, ഡ, ഘ ബ, ഇ, ജ, ഞ, ഛ, ങ, എ, ഏ, ള, ഷ, ഴ, യ, ക, അ, ആ, ഘ, ഝ, ഢ, ഋ

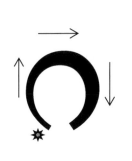

Sound of R as in crush, trust

തറ, പറ, കറ

All consonant letters include the sound of 'A' as in 'cut' unless another vowel is given.

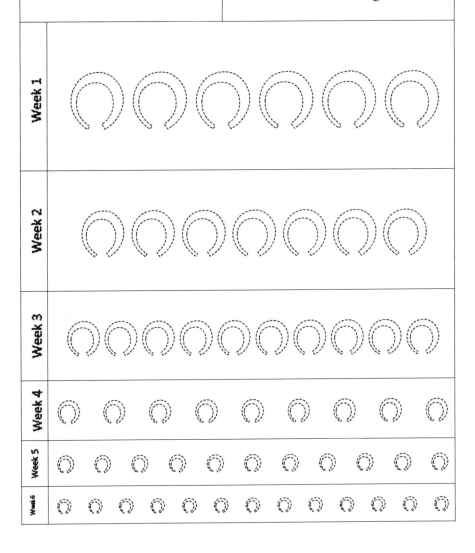

Malayalam Alphabet

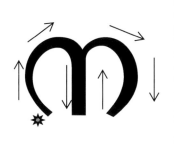

Sound of N as in none, nothing

പന, കനത്ത

It also has another sound for which the tongue needs to touch the teeth.

നല്ല, നാം

Week 1

Week 2

Week 3

Week 4

Week 5

Week 6

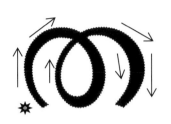

Sound of TH as in thing, path

തല, പത, കതക്

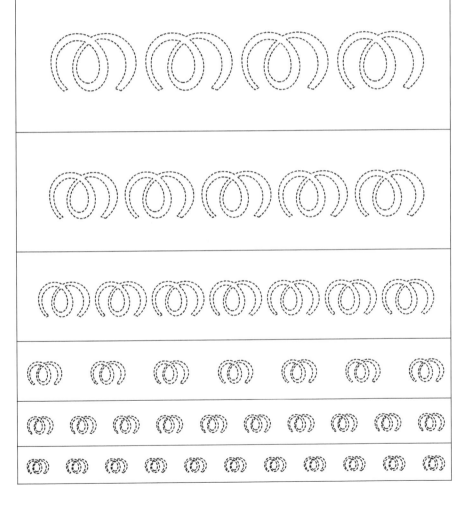

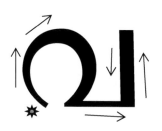

Sound of V as in van, move

വല, വട

Sound of R as in Greek, grace

രാത്രി, കര

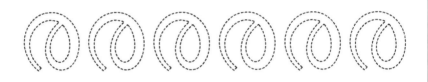

Sound of T as in town, mart

കട, പടം

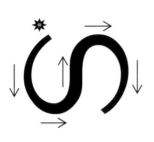

Sound of G as in game, mug

ഗാനം, ഗാന്ധി

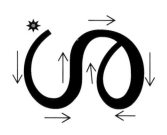

A sound between the sounds of s and sh
Absent in English

ശലഭം, പശ

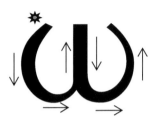

The sound of THE + the sound of H
Absent in English

ധനം, നിധി

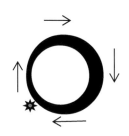

The sound of T + the sound of H
Absent in English

പാഠം, പീഠം

The sound of P as in put, cap

പാഠ, പാഠം

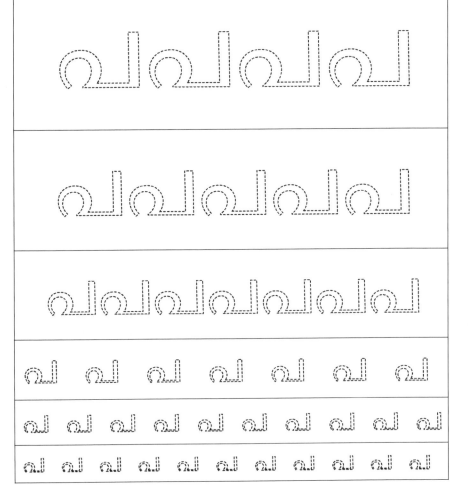

Malayalam Alphabet

The sound of CH as in church, brick

ചാടി, ചീള

Malayalam Alphabet

The sound of DH as in the, that, mother

ദയ, പദവി

Malayalam Alphabet

The sound of B + the sound of H
Absent in English

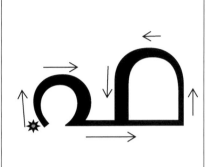

The sound of P + the sound of H
Absent in English

ഫലം, ഫണം

Malayalam Alphabet

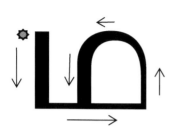

The sound of TH + the sound of H
Absent in English

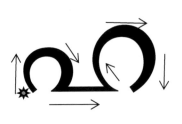

The sound of H as in hat, here

മഹാ, ഹോട്ടൽ

Malayalam Alphabet

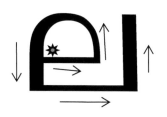

The sound of L as in love, like

മല, കല, പാലം

The sound of M as in man, mouth

മല, മരം, കമല

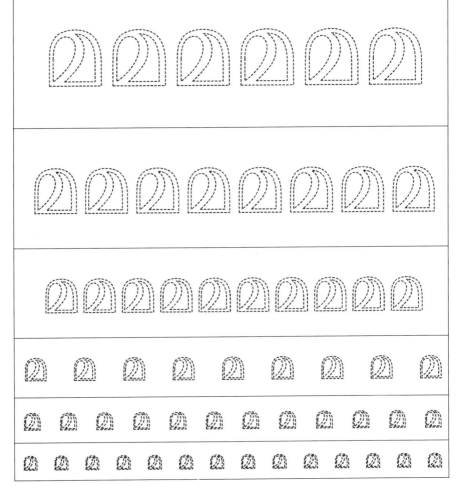

The sound of K + the sound of H
Absent in English

മുഖം, ദുഃഖം

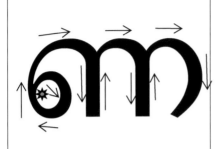

Similar to the sound of N, but the tip of the tongue is moved further back.
As in
money, honey
മണം, പണം

Similar to the sound of O.
as in
call, thought

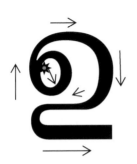

Similar to the sound of U.
as in
put, could

ഉച്ച, ഉറക്കം

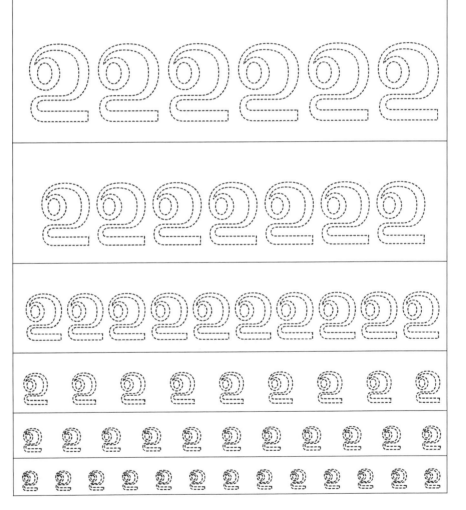

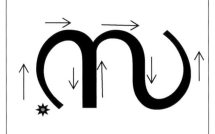

Similar to the sound of S as in
say, sit

സത്യം, സമയം, മാസം

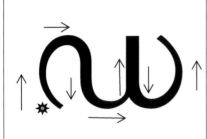

Similar to the sound of D as in
day, do

പീഡ, ഡംഭം

Malayalam Alphabet

Similar to the sound of NG as in sing, thing

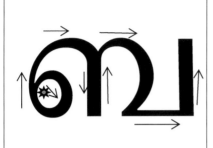

Similar to the sound of B as in
be, cub

ബലം, ബഞ്ച്

Malayalam Alphabet

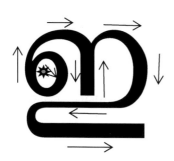

Similar to the sound of I as in
it, sit

ഇത്, ഇന്നലെ

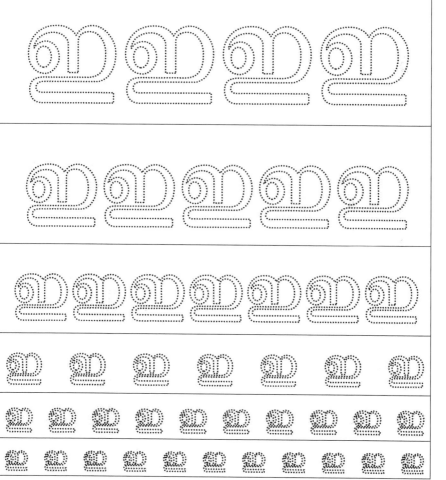

Similar to the sound of J as in
jet, judge

ജയം, ജാതി

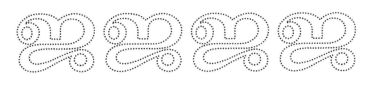

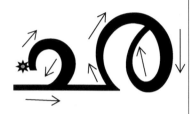

Similar to the sound of CH + the sound of H.

അഛൻ, പുഛരം

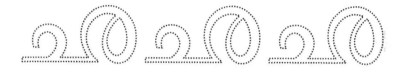

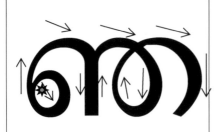

The tongue touches the front to make J sound, and touches the back to make the NG sound. It touches the middle to make this sound. Absent in English.

ഞാൻ, ഞായർ

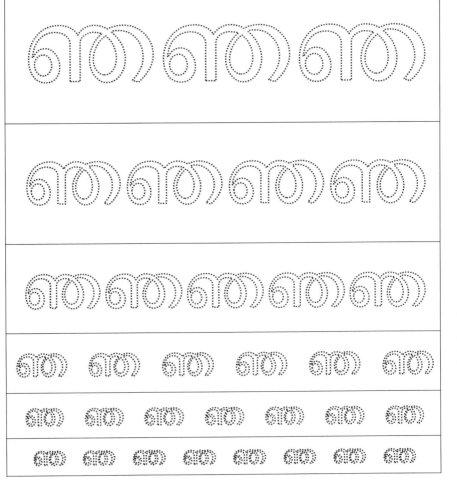

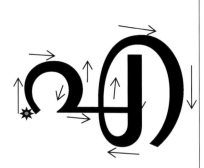

Sound of E as in get, ten

എന്ന്, എനിക്ക്

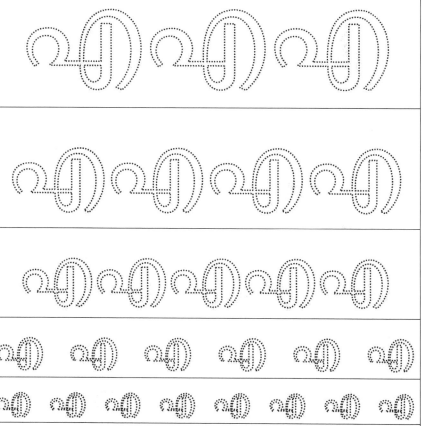

The sound of E made longer.
Absent in English.

ഏട്ടൻ, ഏറ്റവും

Malayalam Alphabet

The sound of L as in clay, blame

കള, തള

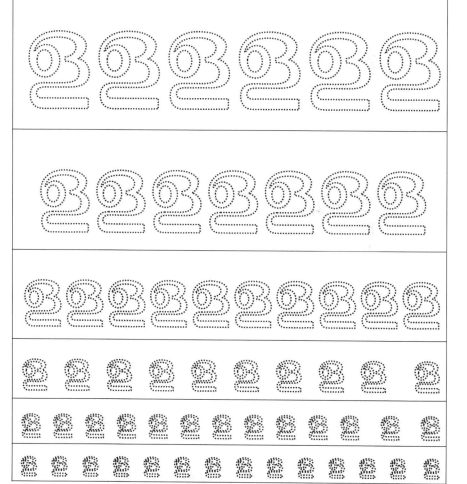

The sound of SH as in shut, bush

മഷി, ഭാഷ

Close to the sound of SH with the tip of the tongue further back.
Absent in English

മഴ, പഴയ

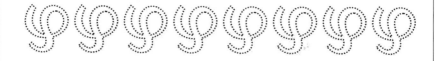

The sound of Y as in yes, your

യാത്ര, കയർ

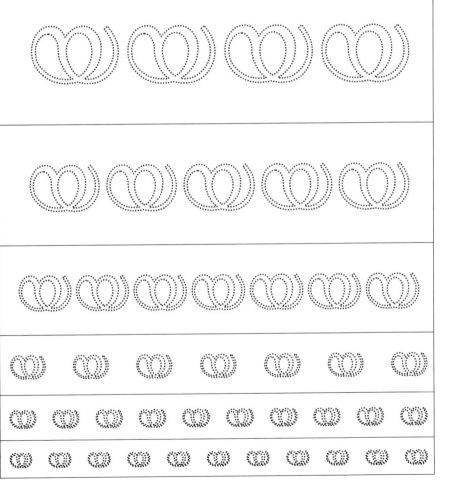

The sound of K as in can, make

കാക്ക, മകൻ

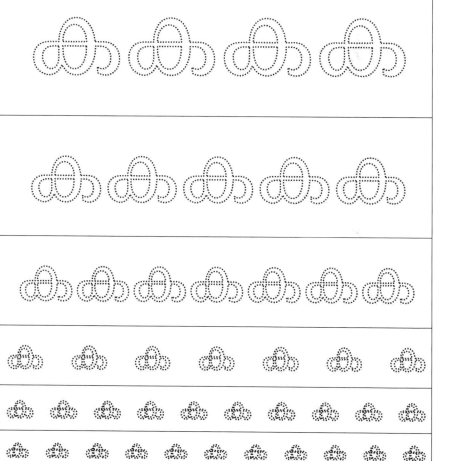

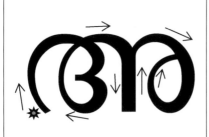

The sound of A as in at, cut

അമ്മ, അത്

Malayalam Alphabet

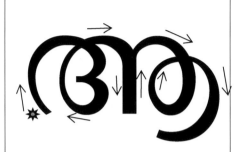

The sound of A made longer as in cart, part

ആന, ആമ

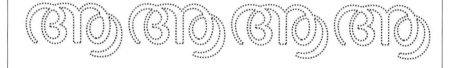

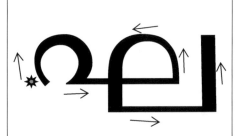

The sound of G + the sound of H
Absent in English

ഘടന, സംഘടന

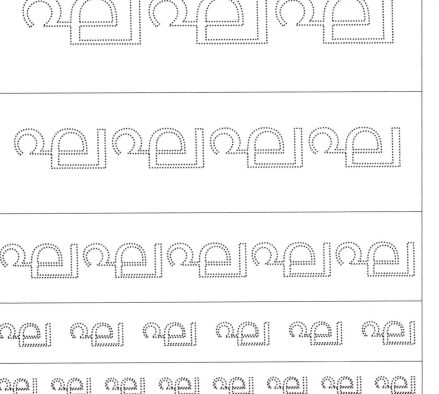

The sound of J + the sound of H
Absent in English, and very rare in Malayalam.

ഡാൻസി

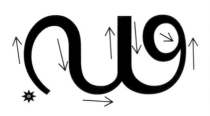

The sound of D + the sound of H
Absent in English

ഗുഡം
മാധ്യം

This occurs only in a few words that have come from Sanskrit. It is listed among vowels, but Malayalees pronounce it like the sound of R.

ഋഷി

ഋഗ്വേദം

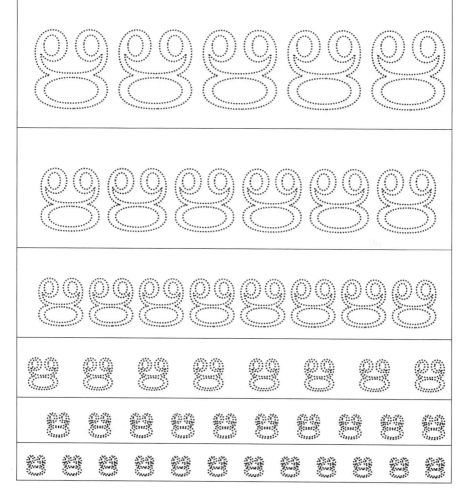

The Short Forms of Vowels

When a vowel stands alone as a syllable, it takes its full form.

അ   ഇ   ഉ   എ   ഒ   ഋ
ആ   ഈ   ഊ   ഏ   ഓ

ഐ   ഔ

But when it stands with a consonant as a part of a syllable, it takes a short form as follows.

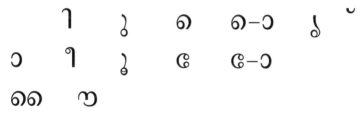

അ does not have a short form, for the consonants have this sound attached with them.

The half-moon sign, ൕ , has no full form, for it never stands alone as a syllable. It serves two functions:
1. It represents a vowel sound as in അത്, കണ്ണ്, മൂക്ക്.
2. It denotes the absence of a vowel with a consonant, as in ക്ട, പ്സ

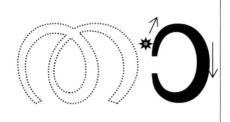

Sound of long A as in cart

Short form of
ആ
കാറ്റ്, പാടി

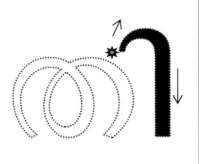

Sound of I as in sit, sip

Short form of
ഇ
കിട്ടി, മിന്നൽ

Sound of long I
as in eat, seat

Short form of
ഈ
മീൻ, വീട്

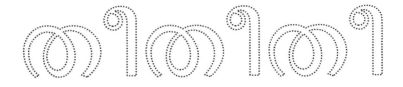

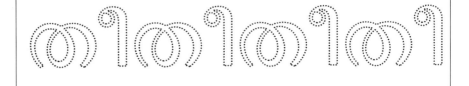

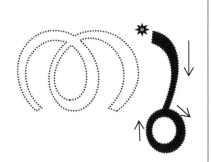

Sound of U as in took, could

Short form of

ഉ

തുണ, കുട

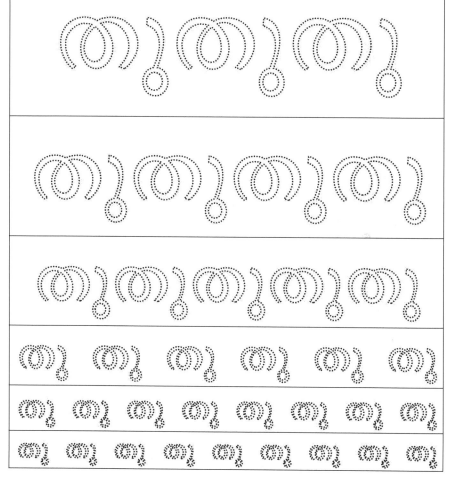

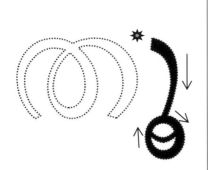

Sound of long U as in Pool, tool

Short form of

ഊ

കൂട്, മൂല

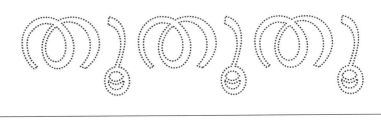

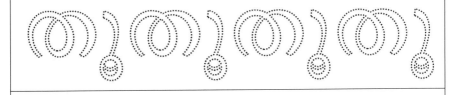

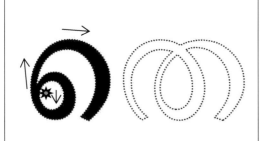

Sound of E as in get, men

Short form of

എ

പെട്ടി, ചെന്നു

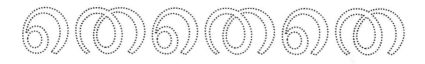

Sound of E as in get made longer

This sound is absent in English. The closest one is the sound of ei as in take.

Short form of ഏ

കേട്ടു, ചേട്ടൻ

Sound of O as in pot, Tom

Short form of ഓ

കൊള്ളാം, പൊന്ന്

Sound of long O as in torn, court

Short form of ഓ

തോമസ്, പോയി

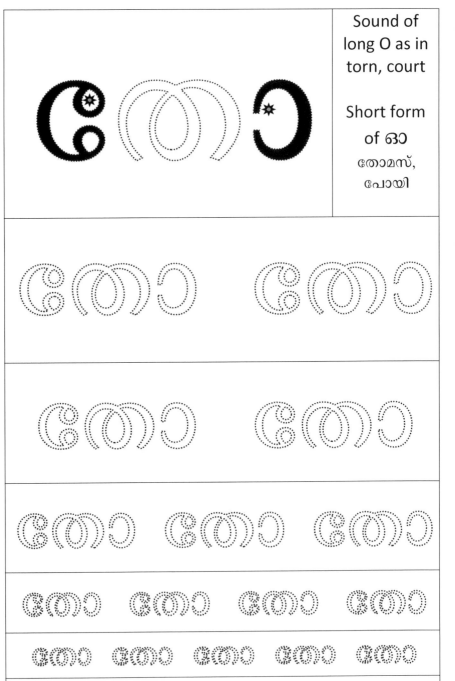

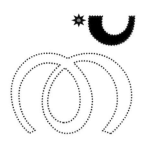

Similar to the underlined sounds in <u>a</u>gain, <u>a</u>head

കപ്പ്, ചീപ്പ്

It also denotes the absence of a vowel with a consonant as in ഷ്ട

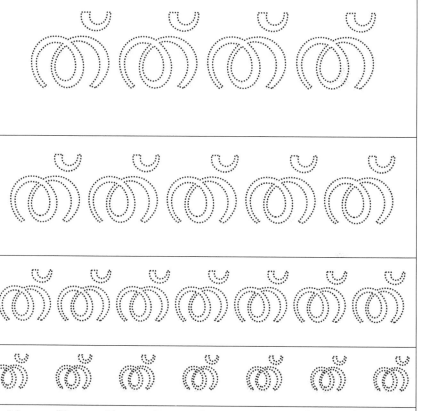

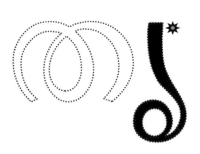

Originally from Sanskrit, Malayalees sound it like R.

Short form of
ഋ

കൃപ, നൃത്തം

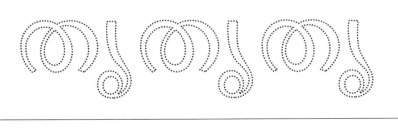

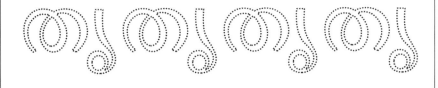

ഐ	Sound of AI or EI as in tile, tale
	Short form of ഐ
	കൈ, ദൈവം

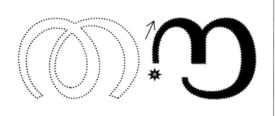

Sound of AU as in town

Short form of ഔ

കൗശലം

Stressed Consonants

Although there is stress in English speech, it is not marked in writing. Seeing the following two words, a foreigner cannot identify the underlined stressed syllables.

Phot<u>o</u>grapher, photogr<u>a</u>phic

But in Malayalam, stress is marked in writing as well. Stressed letters are modified as follows:

Base Form	Stressed Form
ക	ക്ക
ച	ച്ച
ട	ട്ട
ത	ത്ത
പ	പ്പ
ഗ	ഗ്ഗ
ദ	ദ്ദ
ബ	ബ്ബ
ങ	ങ്ങ
ഞ	ഞ്ഞ
ണ	ണ്ണ
ന	ന്ന
മ	മ്മ
യ	യ്യ
ല	ല്ല
വ	വ്വ
സ	സ്സ
ള	ള്ള
	്റ

കക്ക, കാക്ക, മക്കൾ

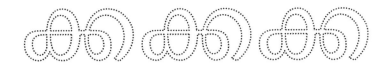

Malayalam Alphabet

പച്ച, കച്ചി

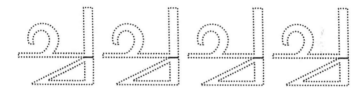

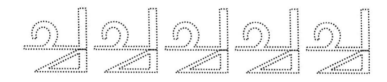

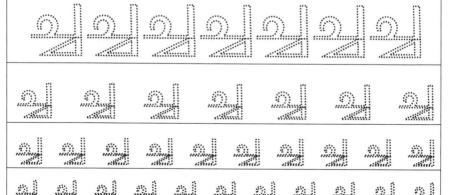

ട

പട്ടി, കട്ട, വേട

 തത്ത, കത്ത്

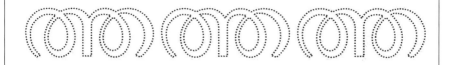

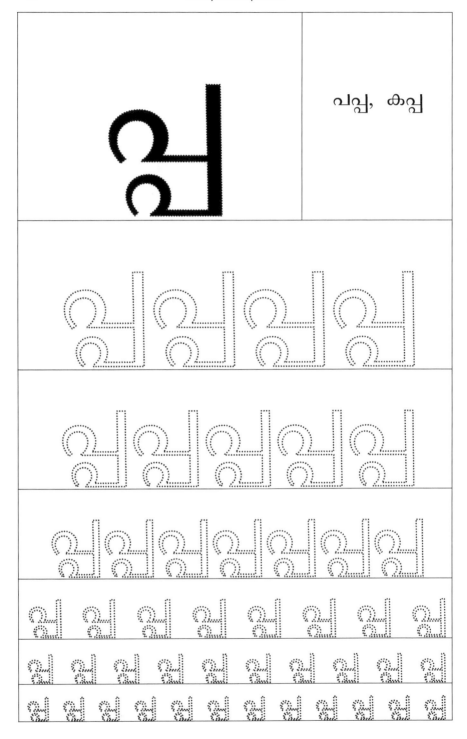

മാർഗ്ഗം, സ്വർഗ്ഗം,

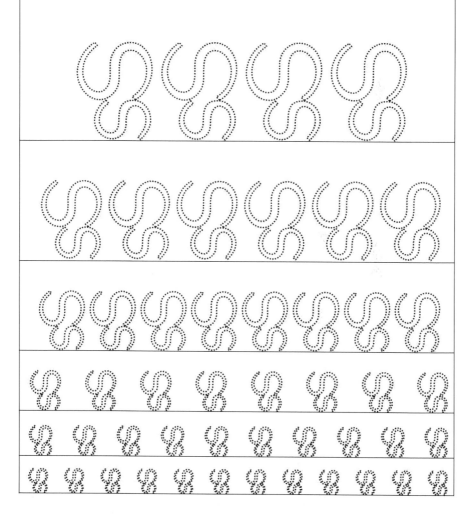

ഭ

അദ്ദേഹം, ഉദ്ദേശം

ക്ലബ്ബിൽ
ഡബ്ബിങ്ങ്

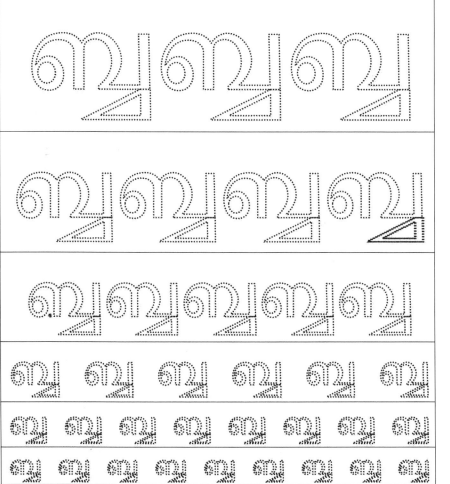

ഭോ

അങ്ങ്, മാങ്ങ

ഞ്ഞാ | മഞ്ഞ, കുഞ്ഞ്

എണ്ണ, കണ്ണ്

This can be sounded in two ways:
Tongue touches the teeth.

Tongue touches the teethridge

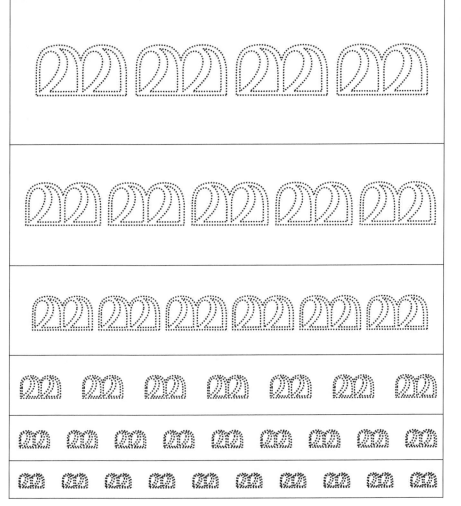

നെയ്യാർ, കയ്യിൽ

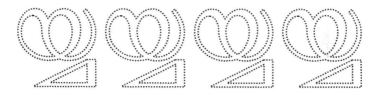

അല്ല, ഇല്ല, പല്ല്

വ്വ

വവ്വാൽ, ഇവ്വിധം

മനസ്സോടെ, തപസ്സ്

ഊ

പള്ളി, വള്ളം

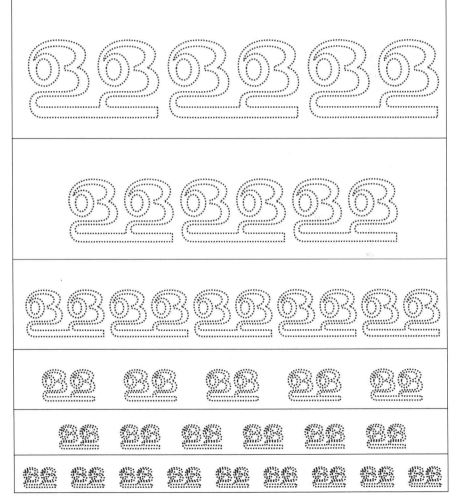

Similar to the sound of t stressed as in sitting

Its base form is  according to its shape, but not according to its sound.

മാറ്റം, തെറ്റ്, കുറ്റം

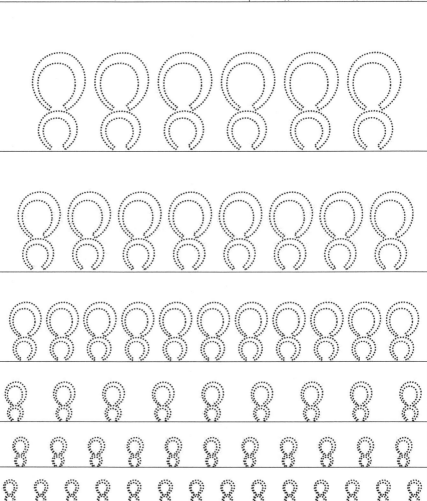

Consonant Combinations

More than one consonant can come together in a syllable. Some of the common combinations are written as follows:

		Combination
ങ്	+ ക	ങ്ക
ഞ്	+ ച	ഞ്ച
ണ്	+ ട	ണ്ട
ന്	+ ത	ന്ത
മ്	+ പ	മ്പ
ണ്	+ ഡ	ണ്ഡ
ന്	+ ദ	ന്ദ
ക്	+ ഷ	ക്ഷ
ത്	+ ഭ	ത്ഭ
ക്	+ ത	ക്ത
ന്	+ റ	ന്റ
സ്	+ ത	സ്ത
ഹ്	+ ന	ഹ്ന
ത്	+ സ	ത്സ

		Combination
ന്	+ ഥ	ന്ഥ
ഗ്	+ ന	ഗ്ന
ന്	+ മ	ന്മ
ണ്	+ മ	ണ്മ
ന്	+ ധ	ന്ധ
ഗ്	+ മ	ഗ്മ
ത്	+ ന	ത്ന
ശ്	+ ച	ശ്ച
ഷ്	+ ട	ഷ്ട
ല്	+ പ	ല്പ
ഹ്	+ മ	ഹ്മ
ജ്	+ ഞ	ജ്ഞ
സ്	+ ഥ	സ്ഥ
ബ്	+ ദ	ബ്ദ

Consonant-combinations can also be written by using the half moon mark of ' ˘ '. When used with this function, this mark shows that the preceding consonant stands without a vowel. Examples:

ക്ത = ക്‌ത,
ത്ഭ = ത്‌ഭ
സ്ഥ = സ്‌ഥ
ഹ്മ = ഹ്‌മ

ങ് + ക

എങ്കിൽ, തങ്കം

ഞ്ച	ങ് + ച
	അഞ്ച്, പഞ്ചം

ണ്ട

ണ് + ട

കണ്ടു, ഉണ്ട്

ന്ത

ന് + ത

പന്ത്, മന്തം

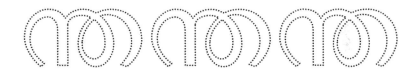

മ്പ

മ് + പ

കമ്പ്, ചെമ്പ്

ണ് + ഡ

ഭാണ്ഡം
ദണ്ഡം

ന്ദ	ന് + ദ
	നന്ദി
	വന്ദനം

ക്ഷ

ക് + ഷ

നക്ഷത്രം
പക്ഷേ

അത്ഭുതം
തത്ഭവം

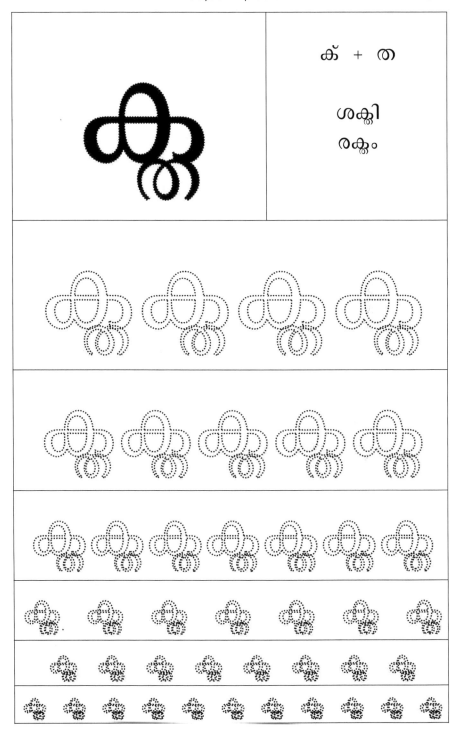

ന് + റ

എന്റെ
അവന്റെ

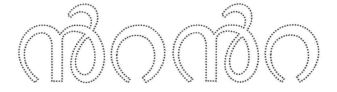

സ് + ത

പുസ്തകം
വാസ്തവം

ഹ്ന

ഹ് + ന

ചിഹ്നം

സായാഹ്നം

ഹ്ന ഹ്ന ഹ്ന

ഹ്ന ഹ്ന ഹ്ന

ഹ്ന ഹ്ന ഹ്ന ഹ്ന

ഹ്ന ഹ്ന ഹ്ന ഹ്ന ഹ്ന

ഹ്ന ഹ്ന ഹ്ന ഹ്ന ഹ്ന ഹ്ന

ഹ്ന ഹ്ന ഹ്ന ഹ്ന ഹ്ന ഹ്ന ഹ്ന

ത് + സ

വാത്സല്യം
വത്സരം

ന് + ഥ

ഗ്രന്ഥം, പാന്ഥൻ

ന്ഥ

ങ് + ന

അഗ്നി
നഗ്നത

ൻ + മ

ന്മ, മേന്മ

ഞ

ണ് + മ

കഞ്മണി

ന്ധ

ന് + ധ

അന്ധത
സിന്ധു

സ് + മ

സ്മ, സിസ്മ

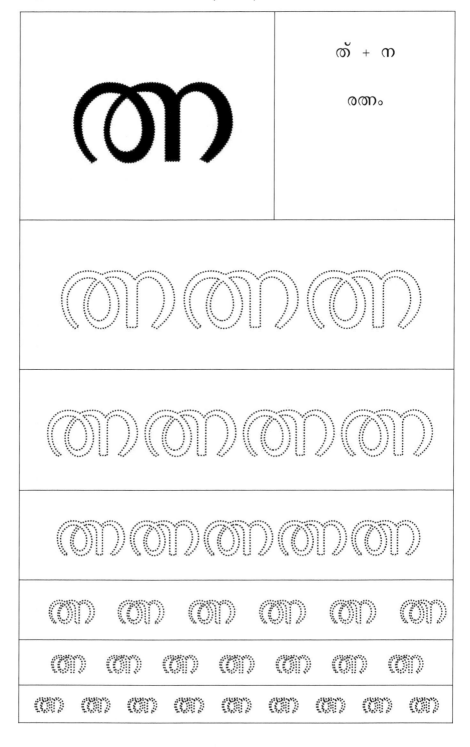

ശ് + ച

നിശ്ചയം
ആശ്ചര്യം

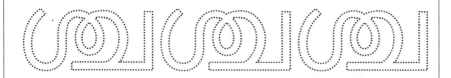

ഷ് + ട

ഇഷ്ടം
നഷ്ടം

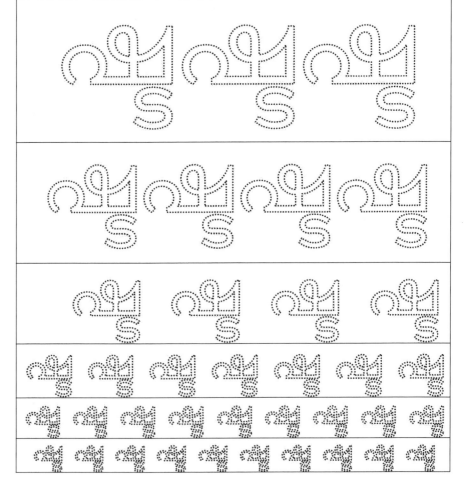

ല് + പ

അല്പം, താല്പര്യം

ഹ് + മ

ബഹ്മം, ബ്രാഹ്മണൻ

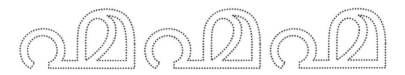

ഇഞ

ജ് + ഞ

ആജ്ഞ
ജ്ഞാനം

സ് + ഥ

സ്ഥലം
ആസ്ഥാനം

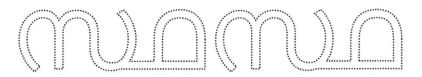

Malayalam Alphabet

ബ് + ദ

ശതാബ്ദം
അബ്ദുള്ള

The Short Forms of Consonants

When two consonants combine, the second one gets transformed to a short form if it is one of the following:

Full Form	Short Form
യ	്യ
ര/റ	്ര
വ	്വ
ല/ള	്ല

Three of them are added at the right side, one at the left side, and one at the bottom.

Example:

ക് + യ = ക്യ
ക് + ര = ക്ര
ക് + വ = ക്വ
ക് + ല = ക്ല

| 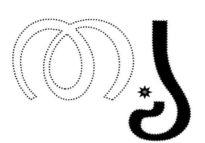 | Sound of Y

Short form of
യ
സത്യം, ലക്ഷ്യം |

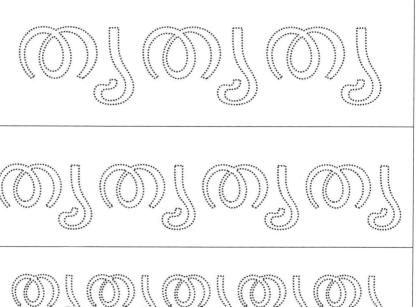

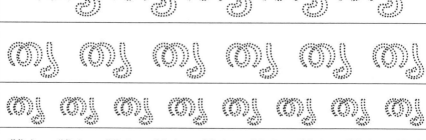

Malayalam Alphabet

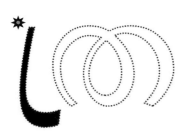

Sound of R

Short form of ○ or ര

ത്രാസ്, ദ്രവ്യം

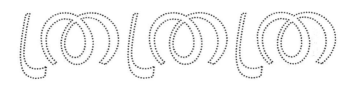

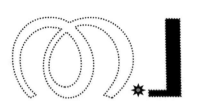

Sound of VA

Short form of വ

തത്വം, മാതൃത്വം

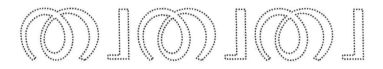

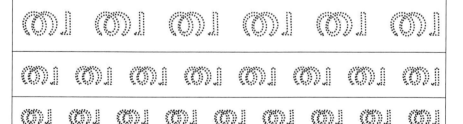

Sound of TH+L

ക്ലേശം, ഗ്ലാനത

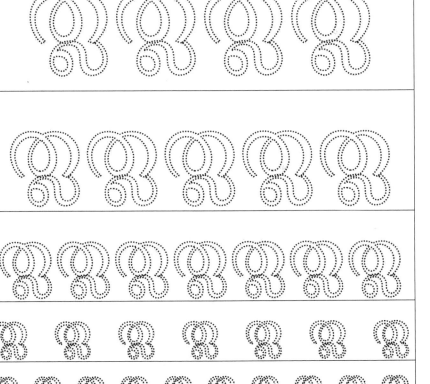

Consonants without a Vowel

When two consonants combine, we have seen how the first one occurs without a vowel as in കട, കപ. But the following consonants can occur without a vowel at the end of words. They don't use the half-moon sign, but get transformed as follows:

With the vowel 'A'	Without any vowel
ന	ൻ
ല	ൽ
ര	ർ
ണ	ൺ
ള	ൾ
മ	ം

This is very common in English. Almost all consonants occur at the end of words in English. Example: cub, Dad, bug, book, them, cup, car, pass, but

But in Malayalam, words mostly end in a vowel sound. Example:
കട, ചെടി, ചെന്നു, എന്നെ, പോയോ, കണ്ട്
If a word in Malayalam does not end in a vowel sound, it must end in one of these: ൽ, ൻ, ൺ, ർ, ൾ, ം.

Sound of ന without vowel sound

അവൻ, മണ്ടൻ

Malayalam Alphabet

Sound of ല
without
vowel sound

കാൽ, പാൽ

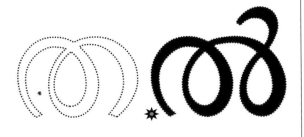

Sound of ഠ without vowel sound

കാർ, അവർ

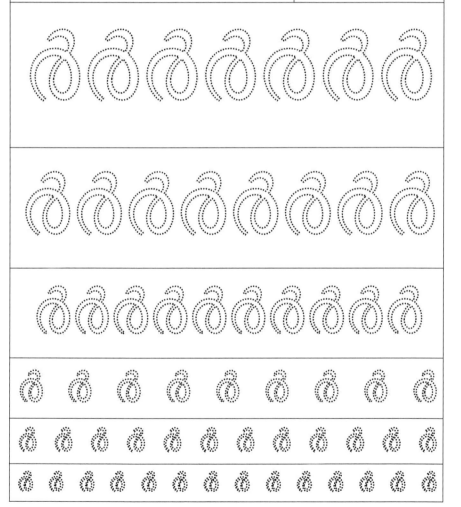

Sound of ണ without vowel sound
പെൺകുട്ടി, മാരത്തൺ

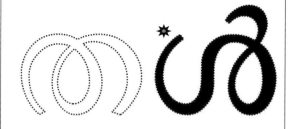

Sound of ള
without vowel sound

അവൾ, കിളികൾ

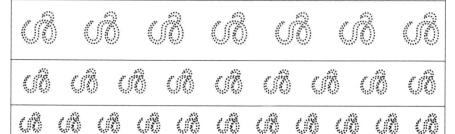

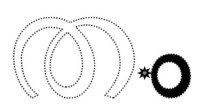

ം without vowel sound

ജനം, കരം, മതം

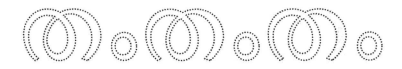

Let us Make Some Words

Read the words in Column B aloud and write them down in column C

A	B	C
elephant	ആന	
bear	കരടി	
horse	കുതിര	
lion	സിംഹം	
pig	പന്നി	
snake	പാമ്പ്	
rabbit	മുയൽ	
fox	കുറുക്കൻ	
donkey	കഴുത	
wolf	ചെന്നായ്	

Read the words in Column B aloud and write them down in column C

A	B	C
eye	കണ്ണ്	
ear	ചെവി	
nose	മൂക്ക്	
tongue	നാക്ക്	
skin	ത്വക്ക്	

Read the words in Column B aloud and write them down in column C

A	B	C
head	തല	
face	മുഖം	
neck	കഴുത്ത്	
chest	നെഞ്ച്	
stomach	വയർ	
leg	കാൽ	
toe	കാൽവിരൽ	
arm	കൈ	
hand	കൈപ്പത്തി	
finger	കൈവിരൽ	

Read the words in Column B aloud and write them down in column C

A	B	C
Cooked rice	ചോറ്	
salt	ഉപ്പ്	
sugar	പഞ്ചസാര	
milk	പാൽ	
food	ആഹാരം	
bread	റൊട്ടി	
tea	ചായ	
coffee	കാപ്പി	
banana	പഴം	
vegetable	പച്ചക്കറി	

Malayalam Alphabet

Read the words in Column B aloud and write them down in column C

A	B	C
house	വീട്	
room	മുറി	
kitchen	അടുക്കള	
Plate	പാത്രം	
scissors	കത്രിക	
table	മേശ	
chair	കസേര	
floor	തറ	
wall	ഭിത്തി	
umbrella	കുട	

Read the words in Column B aloud and write them down in column C

A	B	C
father	പിതാവ്	
mother	മാതാവ്	
brother	സഹോദരൻ	
sister	സഹോദരി	
child	കുട്ടി	
baby	കുഞ്ഞ്	
husband	ഭർത്താവ്	
wife	ഭാര്യ	
Son-in-law	മരുമകൻ	
grandson	കൊച്ചുമകൻ	

Read the words in Column B aloud and write them down in column C

A	B	C
one	ഒന്ന്	
two	രണ്ട്	
three	മൂന്ന്	
four	നാല്	
five	അഞ്ച്	
six	ആറ്	
seven	ഏഴ്	
eight	എട്ട്	
nine	ഒൻപത്	
ten	പത്ത്	

Read the words in Column B aloud and write them down in column C

A	B	C
earth	ഭൂമി	
Sun	സൂര്യൻ	
moon	ചന്ദ്രൻ	
sky	ആകാശം	
sea	കടൽ	
wind	കാറ്റ്	
hot	ചൂട്	
cold	തണുപ്പ്	
river	നദി	
city	പട്ടണം	

Malayalam Alphabet

Read the words in Column B aloud and write them down in column C

A	B	C
big	വലിയ	
small	ചെറിയ	
fat	തടിച്ച	
thin	മെലിഞ്ഞ	
good	നല്ല	
bad	ചീത്ത	
Beautiful	സുന്ദരം	
sweet	മധുരമുള്ള	
bitter	കയ്പ്പുള്ള	
delicious	രുചിയുള്ള	

Read the words in Column B aloud and write them down in column C

A	B	C
black	കറുത്ത	
white	വെളുത്ത	
red	ചുവന്ന	
blue	നീല	
green	പച്ച	
yellow	മഞ്ഞ	
brown	തവിട്ട്നിറമുള്ള	
Dark blue	കടും നീല	
Light blue	ഇളം നീല	

Read the words in Column B aloud and write them down in column C

A	B	C
sat	ഇരുന്നു	
walked	നടന്നു	
ran	ഓടി	
called	വിളിച്ചു	
went	പോയി	
came	വന്നു	
Saw	കണ്ടു	
looked	നോക്കി	
bought	വാങ്ങി	
sent	അയച്ചു	

Read the words in Column B aloud and write them down in column C

A	B	C
week	ആഴ്ച	
day	ദിവസം	
month	മാസം	
Sunday	ഞായർ	
Monday	തിങ്കൾ	
Tuesday	ചൊവ്വ	
Wednesday	ബുധൻ	
Thursday	വ്യാഴം	
Friday	വെള്ളി	
Saturday	ശനി	

Let us Write Some Sentences

I like to learn Malayalam
എനിക്ക് മലയാളം പഠിക്കാൻ ഇഷ്ടമാണ്.

It is the official language of Kerala.
അത് കേരളത്തിൻെറ ഔദ്യോഗിക ഭാഷയാണ്.

It is one of the six classical languages in India.
ഇൻഡ്യയിലെ ആറ് ശ്രേഷ്ഠഭാഷകളിൽ ഒന്നാണ് അത്.

A language in the Dravidian family, this is spoken by about 35 million people
ദ്രാവിഡകുടുംബത്തിൽ പെട്ട ഈ ഭാഷ ഏതാണ്ട് മൂന്നര കോടി ആളുകൾ സംസാരിക്കുന്നു.

Ezuthachan is the father of modern Malayalam.

എഴുത്തച്ഛനാണ് ആധുനിക മലയാളത്തിൻെറ പിതാവ്.

The first Malayalam dictionary was created by Hermann Gundert.

ആദ്യ മലയാള നിഘണ്ടു സൃഷ്ടിച്ചത് ഹെർമൻ ഗുണ്ടർട്ട് ആണ്.

Malayalam vowel letters have two forms: full form when they stand alone, and a short form when they stand with consonants.

മലയാള സ്വരാക്ഷരങ്ങൾക്ക് രണ്ട് രൂപങ്ങളുണ്ട്: ഒറ്റയ്ക്ക് നിൽക്കുമ്പോൾ പൂർണരൂപവും വ്യഞ്ജനാക്ഷരങ്ങളോടൊപ്പം നിൽക്കുമ്പോൾ ലഘുരൂപവും.

The vowel letter 'അ' does not have a short form.
അ എന്ന സ്വരാക്ഷരത്തിന് ലഘുരൂപമില്ല.

The vowel letter of half-moon sign does not have a full form; it has only a short form.
ചന്ദ്രക്കല എന്ന സ്വരാക്ഷരത്തിന് പൂർണരൂപമില്ല, ലഘുരൂപമേയുള്ളൂ.

Some consonant letters also have short form when they combine with others.
ചില വ്യഞ്ജനാക്ഷരങ്ങൾക്കും കൂട്ടക്ഷരമാകുമ്പോൾ ലഘുരൂപമുണ്ട്.

Books by the Same Authors

1. Learn Basic Malayalam in Six Weeks

2. Speak Malayalam in Ten Weeks

After learning the present book, which is level 1, the learner may choose the first one, which is like a level 2. Later the learner may go to the second one, which is level 3.

Both are available in amazon.com.
https://www.amazon.com/John-Daniel-Kunnathu/e/B003FOVYN0

Made in the USA
San Bernardino, CA
25 July 2019